Retracing My Fears

To

Release My Fears

A Journey's Untimely End from Grief and Beyond

Melonie Phillips

Retracing My Tears to Release My Fears:

From Grief and Beyond

Authored by Melonie Phillips

© Melonie Phillips 2021

Cover Design: Marcia M Publishing House Images: Deposit Photos

Edited by Marcia M Publishing House Editorial Team

Published by Marcia M Spence of Marcia M Publishing House,

West Bromwich, West Midlands the UNITED KINGDOM B71 1JB

www.marciampublishing.com

MARCIA M
PUBLISHING HOUSE

DEDICATION

This book is in dedication to my beloved, beautiful
Mom who came into this life singing, dancing and
loving music throughout it all.

Her legacy lives on and on and on…. through her
children, grandchildren and great-grandchildren.
I would like to graciously thank her for loving me
and us and shaping me into the woman that God
wants me to be:
Happy and blessed, through love and sharing
compassion for life towards others. Having the
strength and endurance to do this, blessed to me
from my mother. While she was alive, my Mom had
faced many battles and adversities within sickness
and in health.
Amidst many heartaches, trials and pain, she
showed us love, tenacity, perseverance, humility,
strength and
endurance throughout everything.

She fought on with the grace of a Queen and the agility and strength of a true warrioress.

We are committed to commemorating my beautiful Mom once again, Queen of my heart, Queen of my life.

"THANK YOU."

Retracing My Tears To Release My Fears

A Journey's Untimely End from Grief and Beyond

A Symbol of Endurance and Resourcefulness

Isaiah 40:31 (NIV)

But those who hope in the Lord
will renew their strength.
They will soar on wings like
eagles;
They will run and not grow
weary,
They will walk and not be faint.

Table of Contents

MY MORNING PRAYER

Thank you, Lord, for a peaceful slumber,

To each and everyone one, in many a number,

And for the outpouring of your light all over this
world,

Again, this morning.

Thank you for the recreation of a brand new

dawning and keeping us safe from harm,

Some awakening, some still at rest, allowing us

another chance to do our best.

To convey great kindness, humbleness, love and

care,

To tend to the children, and assist them to

prepare,

And mostly, for always being there.

For the world we live in, and for all we have to do,

For the going out, and being responsible, for all

that we go through.

In our workplace sitting on the bus,
Forgive those who do not know you or seem to
create a fuss.
Help us, Lord, to spread YOUR love,
For keeping us going, by not giving up,
For the lost, the broken, the young and the old,
In this, their story can to you, alone be told.

Gird us, dear Father, hold us tight,
Help us to never lose our sight,
To see and harness our vision, whilst the way is
made clear,
By that remembering, you are always near,
Your mercies enduring,
Your heart filled with LOVE.
The feeling of peace,
Illustrated into the form of a white dove.

Thank you for blessing and choosing me,
And for opening my eyes and enabling me to see,
For not professing to be perfect, but to spread this
message, Each and every morning to the world,
Your children, and to the masses. Amen
God Bless

MOM

You were so cherished by me.

When you were with us

We felt totally free,

At times we would argue and fuss.

If only we knew how important our shared time

would be.

Not knowing the Lord would one day set you free.

Free from all forms of worry,

Removed from all the depths of pain.

To walk with him hand in hand once more,

again and again.

Each day you awakened you spoke to your Lord,

And told him about your burdens and your

heavy load.

For, he knew you were laden and tired with woe

So, he said, "my sweet daughter, it's time to let

go,

To come lay beside me and rest your head on

my chest."

Although we all are lost without you
Our Father knows best.
He gave you a job to take care of yours
Although difficult, you continued on course.
With sickness upon you
And daily pain,
You tended to your children again and again,
You loved us unconditionally
Your grand ones too.
Without you Queen,
We are unsure what we should do.
All I pray is that you get your rest,
No more pain and no more stress,
No more to worry about us.
I hope on that day,
Not to miss that last bus,
To catch it on time, early and not late,
So that I can meet you at the pearly gate.
So, we can hold each other tightly again,
And let my tears fall onto your shoulder,
After that, for me, life shall be over.
Thankful shall I be for my beautiful Mom
Yes, I am.

I will ever let go until The Lord himself says I can,

He knew that you were laden,

And tired with woe,

So,

He said, "my Sweet Daughter, it's time to let go

to come lay beside me rest your head on my

chest."

We all are lost without you,

But our Father knows best...

THE BARREL OF DISTRESS

Sometimes life can be a massive mess
When we find ourselves in the 'barrel of
distress.'
Striving to get to the top after falling down a
massive drop.
Whether it is in death, divorce, heartache and
pain.
Is there a choice to leave or remain?
Climbing up daily with your family to care for
Still with the heaviness of heart on the floor.
Two steps forward, fifty steps back.
At times feeling defensive from this massive
attack.
The heart is wounded susceptible to an
abundance of pain
The steps have to be slow ones in order to heal
No one can dismiss the way you feel
This is the life we have we need to keep it real!

Keep on climbing holding onto the safety rope

Each day you awake that equates to hope.

This barrel of distress is a temporary place

Gather your strength and endeavour.

To remove yourself from this space

Taking your time, no need to haste.

As the time will surely come

With a steady, manageable pace

No need to run.

Setting yourself free.

Coming from within is difficult to believe

But if you endure, you shall surely achieve.

RISE OF THE MORNING SUN

A touch of heaven, watching the rising of the
morning sun.
Not an experience, just for fun.
Truly a blessing conveyed from Mother Earth
In line with the wonder of a new birth.
A newness of life every day,
Gifted to us, in such a special way.

If only we could take a moment to review
all the blessings that are all around, bursting
into view.
Birds singing softly, in the trees,
The subtle touch on faces, of a gentle warm
breeze.
The Ladybirds, with red hot wings,
resting on the garden wall.
To listen when the Fox cubs call.

The quiet buzzing of the black and yellow
Honeybee.
What a wonderful, impressive sight to see.

When we blow our breath on the Dandelion puff
flower,
And visualise the white parachutes that occupy
the small child for hours and hours.
Amidst an array of Buttercup yellow flowers,
A touch of heaven is in this place,
We would notice if we were not in so much of a
haste.
The Butterfly flutters vibrant and colourful wings,
And if we listen keenly, we can hear the
Blackbird as she sings.

To see the rise of the morning sun once again,
Today is a brand new one, so let us embrace
and be truly thankful, for this morning is not the
end.
It is a new beginning.

GONE TOO SOON

Your life had just begun,

Living for you seemed like so much fun.

Vibrant, happy, beautiful and free,

Journeying through life the way life should be.

Not too many worries with an abundance of cares;

I heard friends say you were always there.

They could count on you.

You would have their back too.

Many felt blessed on hearing that.

I wake up each day and feel to curse,

As I remember your name, engraved into your

casket,

through the glass windows of the hearse.

To ask them why they cut your life short

And chose to break so many hearts.

So now we weep and now we mourn,

For our dear Joel to his family, he was born.

To say a prayer, and your Mom to kiss you Goodnight,

For you are no longer in our sights.

The lights are dim, our hearts are too,

You're loved by all.

Your siblings know not what to do.

For you are not here, we feel such loss,

What a price to pay; we cannot count the costs.

In loving memory of Joel Richards May 2018

THE SCENT OF YOU

I pressed my face into your pillow today,
I wanted to smell the scent of your Eau de
parfum spray.
I hear myself screaming from inside,
'cause you left me in this way.
There is a piercing pain inside my brain.
I want you back,
I need you near,
I can't see your face,
I can't hear your voice in my ears,
I don't have a choice, subjected to my own fear.

Standing on top of a mountain peak with grief,
I still cannot accept or maybe still in disbelief,
Undoubtedly, in a full state of shock,
As I adapt to this life that has abruptly stopped,
No longer there, you were my rock.
The world is quickly spinning out of my control,
I need to get off,

If only to preserve my soul,

My heart and its pieces are on the floor.

Seemingly, I don't want to face anything

anymore.

My world will stop as the heartache demands,

And the life I knew will crumble into grains of

sand.

I seek your scent, the aroma of you,

Reminiscing on your fragrance still carries me

through.

A MOTHER'S TRUE LOVE

A Mother's true love can never be compared to
any love, anywhere.

Except for the love of our Creator

A Mother's love can always be shared equally

Amongst her daughters and her sons,

Fathers and brothers and sisters too.

This comprehension is too great to compare

That the loss of this love is way too much to bear

Especially when that Mother's love can no
longer be there.

Oooooooooooooh the pain.

DEATH OF A YOUNG ONE

Death of young one,
So brutal so cruel,
We send our youth dem
To learn at school,
So why do they do this?
Do they not talk?

Why the bloodshed? Can't they just walk?
There is a code when
one of the man dem gone,
Is it heartache, misery, stress and pain?
Or to hurt one another indiscriminately
and mash-up Mommas aim?

To grow her offspring on this Mother Earth,
To contribute to society and to know their worth,
That they were once Kings and Queens,
Prince and Princesses living life so serene.

It is difficult to know that place,

As sometimes, they are looked at in such disgrace.

So as their elders, let's show their truth,

What their lives are worth to me and you.

They are our blessing from God above,

A gift to be embellished with pure, clean love,

We are not perfect; we get things wrong,

But let's not use excuses, we don't have too long.

*In Loving Memory of all of our young people who have
lost their lives through crime*

SISTER HOW I MISSED YA!

I saw you today, you looked into my eyes,
From when our Mom passed away,
we said our last goodbyes.
For me, that was tragic and so unfair,
I did not fathom, when Mom left to go to heaven,
you would not be there.

To share our journeys, to express our shared pain,
I realised the grief for me, was again and again
and again.
No Brothers, no Sister, no Niece, no Mom,
On that March day, you all had gone.

All left together, left in vain,
I have more to say but choose to refrain.
My heart's been broken so many times,
But did not know, you would all be gone,
and I would be left alone on the vine.

So cruel, uncaring, and unkind,
You all knew you would leave me behind,
That one day, you would set yourselves
Free, from your sister... yes, that is me!!!

I will bow out gracefully,
I will take my leave because
only God alone can regrow this seed,
To bring new roots of togetherness as we grieve.

This family seed had been planted by our Mom,
I hope she does not know the fruit of this, now she
has gone.
Seems you have all forgotten,
Our times together in Spencer Way,
When we used to ramp together and happily, laugh
and play,
Our Mom was there, you know so too.
Now, there should not be me without you.

NEED TO SEE YOU AGAIN

Pangs of guilt, a deepness of pain

I am in need to see you again

Only now I envision you in my dreams

When I'm awakened your face, I can't even see

The guilt I feel now that you are gone

There was still so much left to do... I remember

Mom!

The pain still lingers way too deep

Often, I cry myself to sleep

Wondering why you're not there

People around me don't really seem to care

The guilt I feel now that you are gone

There was still so much left to do... I remember

Mom!

EMPRESS TEARS
THIS JOURNEY IS TO BE
ENDURED

Empress, don't cry, wipe the tear from your eye,
Relax and do not stress.
You must embrace life where possible,
remove all vibes of negative-ness,
From out of your serene space.
To encourage the fullness of grace to take place,
Absorb all the beautification of nature through
the pores of your skin, within
Covering your face with hands adorned in
delicate silk lace.
Stand firm and hold your ground,
When time, life and its enemy attacks, come to
hold you down.
For you shall retain your jewel-encrusted crown,
Remember you are blessed with a sheer inner
joy, consigned with a lifetime supply.

The mother of all nature.

Your womb has been blessed uniquely by our Creator,

For only, you can shape life, that is greater,

A man-child or woman-child,

Ever so meek and mild.

Hold your offspring for whether it's a girl or a boy, given to you to love and deploy,

To enhance, nurture and gird them strong,

To live on the earth all their days long.

With the Love of a King Man Warrior and Empress Queen,

To seek to join hands.

To join together in Holy harmony and reign supreme,

Into the unification and oneness of (wo)mankind.

This role for you has been destined,

Hold your head up, set your shoulders, straight towards the wind, Blessed with the finer things.

For this mission, you have been chosen,

The fullness of joy and perfumed essence this will bring.

At the journey's end, you shall shine, radiant
and bright.
With gold embossed and in full sight.
Although trials and tribulations are at full mast,
You will not be the first and definitely never
need to be the last.
So, Empress, don't you cry,
Wipe the tears from your eyes,
At times there are revelations in life, amidst
great waves of strife,
But you shall not succumb to them, whether day
or night,
You shall not be lost, within the torrential storm,
For every day, a child, to an Empress Queen is
born.
You shall shelter the babe, from the sting of harm,
For after the tyrant storm, the place will become
gently calm.

FIRST MOTHERING SUNDAY WITHOUT YOU 2016

On Mothering Sunday last, I was loved, happy
and carefree,
just for the mere fact, my Mother was here with
me.
Smiling, laughing and feeling blessed,
not foreseeing what was around the corner, the
Tsunami, wave of stress.
That tomorrow my Mama would be laid up in
bed,
not knowing the journey ahead, was out of our
hands
because our beautiful Mama, Nanny and Friend,
was on the road to her journey's end.
Unknowing, unforeseen we didn't have a clue,
To realise we were going to lose you,
Our great Mother, our great Queen,
On you, we can always depend.
So, on this Mothering Sunday, I think of you,

Oh Mom, now for a whole year, I have
continued without you.
Not in my own strength, an inner strength that
has been guided by Him,
He has held me tightly together from deep within.
So, as we put flowers down where you lay,
We continue daily to pray,
To think and to dream of you, constantly
missing you, as we get through.
Oh, Mom, I am waiting patiently to see your face.
I await to see you in my dreams,
So that clearly in my mind,
I know that you are resting PEACEFULLY...

THE SUN SHALL RISE ONCE AGAIN TOMORROW

The sun shall rise once again tomorrow,
So that one can heal from an ensemble' of
sorrow,
This passage may seem dark and the
proceedings grim,
Kick back and tattoo on a 'cheesy grin.'
The mood mostly can seem time-sensitive and
bleak,
Rendering your lips sealed; not to open, to speak.
At times, the darkness seems to have no end.
Take a walk, phone a friend,
The sun shall rise the very next day,
Remember to open your eyes, smile, then to pray
For you had hoped to see another one,
Although your loved one has passed on,
The wounds shall heal, knitting the heart back
together,

And memories will live on, forever and ever,

The clock will keep ticking and hourly chime.

These darker days shall, one day, decline.

The hope of rising up from out of the dust,

On you after time shall be pleasantly thrust,

For time shall be your greatest healer,

This time stood still can be the wealthiest stealer,

Take the time to watch the sunrise,

To live in the legacy of your loved ones, not

accepting the dark demise.

ON MY LIFE'S JOURNEY

If my life could start all over again
I would ask the Lord to be my closest friend
From the very beginning to the very end
To know of no heartache, to feel no pain
Just to captivate the beauty of life again and again

To know not fear, to never know woe
Being constantly at ease and going gently with
the flow
Blessing of countless family and of great friends
An abundance of joy until the end
Awakening with the love for others on my lips
To tip toe through the tulips, swinging my hips

Without a worry with not a care
To share this gift of life with the people who
were there
Whether man, woman, boy or girl
To see this spreading throughout the world

To see no colour to show care for no particular
creed
Not to worry about wealth or participation for
greed

To give onto to others what God gave to you.
To choose the positivity of being happy and free
With the guarantee that there is a God-
An inspired planned out journey especially for me

Today is the first day
Showing grace and beauty when you can
This is the positives of man and woman
Not taking the negative stereotypes on board
Has this will cause a mind overload
Taking care of family and supporting friends
This shows a woman of virtue until the very end.

Sometimes there is confusion
At times there is great loss
Rest assured God is with you
For He is the boss

Always give honour and glory
Onto Him alone
Let him in to change you from the outside to
within
Today is the first day
So let us begin.

GRIEF

An unknown road,

An isolated place,

A darkened inclusion,

To be taken at a go-slow pace...

Is this the norm?

A stranger to this place,

Looking into the mirror,

I cannot see or recognise my own face...

The lights growing increasingly dim,

The world's spinning unequally cold,

No longer can I see my loved one,

Neither bought nor sold,

Is this my own journey?

Or own self-made grief,

Are you trying to steal my soul?

Like a downright thief,

To kill, to destroy me,

Is that your aim?

I shall not let you control me

If I do not allow you a name.

My heart is heavy,
A flood with pain,
Upon your strength Father,
I will remain,
To you the glory, the one that stands,
Not giving into painful demands.
So, I will close my eyes,
And clasp my hands,
Cause when I have fallen,
In your footprints,
I will stand.
So, when it's dark,
and I feel so scared,
I will continue to ask you,
To keep me prepared
For this heart of mine is
So deeply scarred,
Is this my ill-gotten pain?
Trying not to give in,
Underneath the strain,
On this darkened journey, at times,
I have been blamed.

So, I shut my door and lock myself in,

For now, my prayer

is for real transformation and healing to begin...

From an unknown road, an isolated place,

a darkened inclusion at a gentle pace.

ANTICIPATING OUR EXIT

Anticipating our end,
So deep in thought, not wading shallow,
The concept of this eventuality,
makes us feel hollow.
We may at times choose to overlook this,
Wondering where we will go,
The thought of our end is way
too deep to swallow or defend.

Each family dynamic locks this out,
When the end forces its way in,
We realise what this is all about.
Amidst turmoil and confusion and much pain,
Too much to bear,
A harsh jolt, on that day when it comes,
It's here to remain.

Trying to raise the subject over dinner,
Your food can get stuck on this taboo subject,
Not wanting to ponder or reflect,
A concept we choose to reject,
No not easy to simmer.

No one wants to face it,
Not ever, not right now.
Shut this one down,
Heartless!! Who? Me? How?
To discuss a will or details of the order of service,
For less disagreements,
It is truly worth it.
Unfortunately, we shut the door,
Standing firmly not wanting to hear any more,
Who forgot?
Pleading for discussion,
For the anticipated day which will eventually
come,
Whatsoever else maybe, on this dreaded day,
we shall all see the requirements could be simple,
A need to write them down,
On the spot, a full desire to wear a frown,
So, the dreaded occasion can be sorted
Without the need for messing about,
Trying to fathom what
You don't understand; your loved one will have
Taken all this planning into their hands.

More time can be spent together,
Shaping new and old memories forever,
Taking time out to allow
Your anticipation to run and remain free....
For whatever the exit shall be, Will be...

HURT AMIDST A FLOOD OF PAIN

Hurt amidst a flood of pain
Can aim to incarcerate one's weary brain,
Where once there was love
Now stands an intensity of pain,
That can linger on stronger, for years to remain.

The shock waves of doubt
That can resonate within man,
Was the plan of the enemy
To bring about the downfall of the human?

The battle is on, the struggle is real
There is only one voice that can combat how
one feels,
For the Holy Trinity, the Great I am
The wonderful counsellor, who walked in Zion,
To eliminate the hurt amidst the floods of pain
so, for this great controversy,
No longer to stay the same.

STRESS

You are a killer, a heart chiller.

That is what you are!!!

Holding onto someone way too tight,

You have gone too far.

Showing up in someone's psyche,

uninvited late at night,

Pairing yourself with anxiety,

Difficult to explain your lack of sobriety.

The two of you together are a real distress to

one's brain, loaded together with blood pressure

and pain.

Shot up high, becoming overwhelmed, as though

you could reach the sky.

Feeling well thwarted, nerves are a mess,

We shall no way undermine

What you are capable of, with your own dreaded

distress, needing to relax and take a rest,

'cause with you onboard, we do not feel at our
best.
A well-deserved dance-filled weekender
A sun-filled rest upon a cool veranda,
This seems a great way to demolish the
conundrum,

Take up the offer and put this into your plan,
to remove this STRESS from the psyche,
and 'carpe vita' {seize the life},
or 'carpe diem' {seize the day},
Just because you can!!...

ON DEEP REFLECTION

Knowledge subdued at the depth of the seas,

A deep sense of yearning for the great one

supreme.

Without the need for school or college,

Not only in university do we OBTAIN

knowledge.

An accolade of learning received from mother

nature,

this is meant to be for the greater.

Considering the entirety of our surroundings,

on a day like today

With a willingness to learn, love and dream and

to pray.

With the serenity of deep meditations,

to harken the spirit, attuned to life's unique

vibrations,

With no time to worry or carry any deepness or

fearful citations,

With no time to ponder why we are here!

Realising that there must be a great purpose and
such a grand plan,
Gained from the wonders and knowledge and
Greatness of one, a supreme being untouched by
man.
With knowledge of self-awakening by
uncontrollable dreams,
Halt for a minute take a moment to breathe.
Utilise the sounds around you to embrace
this intense feeling, hearing the musical
interludes of this space, Exploring the depths of
the time you are in,
with thanks and grace.
All intensified by mother nature's warmth,
harnessed from the core within.
On deep reflection of this magnificent place,
how do we give thanks, where do we begin?
Can we fully over - stand the life that we are
living?

UPLIFTING ONE'S PEOPLE
DAY BY DAY

Uplifting one's people day-by-day,
Erasing negativity installed along our life's way,
Creating and empowering,
never forgetting to pray,
Enlightening ourselves and remembering
lost ancestors along our way.
Never forgetting them who opened the doors for
tomorrow,
subjected to years of unprovoked sorrow.

Still to keep a smile upon your face,
Although the road can be rough, and it feels like
a fight daily takes place.
Standing up for the right, to discredit the wrong,
Singing quite loudly, a beautiful song.

Always remember, the rough times will not be
here long,
Constantly speaking life, into one's people.
day after day,
Never allowing doubt to uproot and darken your
way,
Upliftment and power to the people.
Fists together to show all we are equal,
Uplifting one's people day-by-day,
Erasing negativity installed along life's way.

STORM CLOUDS LOOMING

The storm clouds are over me once again,

Must be a sworn enemy, surely not a friend.

Standing up, then knocked down with a great

thud, unto the ground.

Hear the echoes, feel the sound,

Needing to remove an almighty weight from off

your shoulders.

Being aware of the effects of this cloud,

As you are getting older.

Firmly it takes a tightened grip of the mind,

at times almost driving all insane from inside.

The control is slowly diminishing, to say the

least,

Attacking and raging like a ferocious beast.

Chopping and changing at will,

There is a great need

to stop, drop and chill,

No more blood leftover to spill.

These emotions cannot be explained,

Thoughts damaging to the cells of the brain.

Overwhelmed and feeling so lost,

Seems so unfair at such a cost.

With the clouds hovering, impacting, harshly
over this life,

Emotional feelings are not always wrong or right.

Wondering if this is a burden or an ill-gotten fate?

Seeking to love today, holding great pain
tomorrow,

Taken on abruptly to harbour self-hate,

At this present place in life, filled with many
sorrows,

Taking all burdens onboard,

With hopes of brighter tomorrows.

Thankful to friends and family, glad to see me
here,

Continuing to face the dark,

looming clouds of my very own fear.

YOU CLOSED YOUR EYES

You closed your eyes and left this earth,
I went to speak to the professionals for what it's
worth,
Whose job I thought was to enable us to see
Instead, they set you free.

Every day all we could do was watch, wait and
pray.
Your journey in this world was never easy,
In my humble opinion, you left us way too early.

The tubes, the wires around your bed,
For us to see, sent pain waves through my head,
The monitors' signals shooting up and down,
All we could do was stand, stare, and just look
around.

Watching you there, I imagined peacefully asleep,
But at the time, most definitely, to all-out defeat,
The sight to see, sending shockwaves through
my head,
For you were preparing for your road ahead.

We carry this burden a heavy load,

If only I had known you were going home

And leaving us here, all alone.

I would have kissed you and hugged you much more.

Told you I loved you much more than before.

I would have bid you a beautiful goodnight.

And said, "Mum have a safe, smooth and peaceful flight."

...From Marnin with love x...

MY HERO

You are my <u>HERO,</u>
Mum, that is who you are,
It has taken for me to lose you,
For me to see that,
Now that you have gone away, so far.
I noticed your courage each day,
With all that life threw, you combatted in every
way.
Your journey was never easy, whilst you were
here,
And at times stress would take hold,
But you were forever brave and outright bold,
Showing no fear.
You always embraced this life with both of your
hands,
And always tried your best,
Not giving in to life's high demands.
The beauty you had shined inside and out,
Increased with age, without a doubt.
You turned life over gracefully, from page to page,

The strength of your character taking centre
stage,
For us mere mortals, we were utterly amazed,
Your love for all, trust me, has set our hearts
ablaze.
But you became weary within this rat race,
Steadily, having to take life at a slower pace.
We have inherited your strength, that you had left,
For us to live on without you, with this gift, we
are blessed.
You still amaze me through and through,
We still have your love when we are struggling
without you.
Your glistening beauty,
And ultimate charm,
To this very day inside of me, with thoughts of
you,
I feel comfort and warmth.
Although this life has been daunting and
sometimes a blast,
You needed to allow yourself freedom from the
haunting past.

You are my <u>HERO</u>,

MUM, most definitely you are,

There would be NO me without you, that is so true,

You are my <u>HERO</u>,

Mum, that is what you are.

It took for me to lose you, for me to see that,

Now that you have gone away, so extremely far.

ALWAYS A FIGHT IN THE WRESTLING RING OF LIFE

The cushioned gloves are on,
in the wrestling ring of life,
The reinforcements are surrounding one.
Sometimes defensive, other times wrong,
Keeping things together, forever staying strong.
The mind is wondering, within your ups and
downs,
Not always a fun person to be around.
Even when the fight has finished, still the true
emotions show,
Fully diminished, still trying not to let it go.
Always alert in the battle zone, fighting on
feeling all alone,
Dressed, armoured in battle attire,
Ready to put out any ferocious fire.
At times, a softened approach will be needed,
But the defensiveness sometimes superseded.
The wall of doubt has been built,

The heart filling with blood which can then be spilt, a succession made from columns of guilt.
You are roughed up in the ring and then coated in filth,
Parading within the wrestling ring of life,
Whether with husband, children, friend, or wife.
Preparing for what lies ahead,
Visualising that you could end up dead,
Still wrestling with the cushioned gloves on.
One day you need to take them off, to move on.
As this way of life comes, with heartache, at an increasing cost, rendering your spirit to become lost.
Pressured thoughts that when there is a cause to fight,
You quickly put your armour back on to settle the score,
Sadly, stepping back into the wrestling ring of life once more.
Dressed, armoured in battle attire,
Ready to put out any ferocious fire.

SOMETHING

.... broke into my life the other day,

And you wouldn't leave. You wanted to stay.

I needed for you to go away,

You slipped under my bedroom door, into my

darkened room, around my mind, heart, and

body you decided to swoon.

You are so dreaded coming in at such a cost,

For you know, I had recently suffered a great

loss,

But that is how you try and take control of one's

mind, body and enter the depths of the soul.

Firstly, infiltrating the mind, then spreading to

the body.

How is it your so bold?

Your whole approach is way too shabby,

To take and destroy someone's soul,

For them to feel trapped on the whole.

But guess what .... I will be letting you go.

Just politely wanted to let you know,

That you and I are no more.

I am through with you,

It's over, I said, I can see that you just wanted me dead,

How dare you encroach yourself into my life?

I am a mother, a friend, a sister and a wife.

My time and life are way too full,

For your nonsense, to take effect and pull.

So, I am now relinquishing my association with you.

As I said before, we are done, we are through!!

I am not saying it will be easy, but I must try.

I cannot take any more, having no more tears I want to cry,

It is time for me to say goodbye.

DEPRESSION...There is no more you and I,

MY SOLDIERESS BEAUTIFUL EMPRESS

You showed yourself to be a beautiful
Soldieress.
You showed all your full composure as a
beautiful Empress,
Under an abundance of great distress.
Adorning pure elegance nothing less,
Daily for months doing your absolute best,
Showing the world, throughout devastation,
that you are blessed,
Watching you feeling tired, needing to rest,
A true warrior Empress.
Creating Love within your own distress,
Looking after everyone with the shield of
righteousness not to impress,
Self-less to the end, watched by God and your
friends,
Looking out and praying for you and your family
too.

Recognising that you are all truly blessed,
Your wealth of compassion never rationed,
You show yourself approved all the way,
Your kindness is always on display.
Although you are so deeply hurt,
And your own heart has been torn through your
shirt,
On each and every side, within every single
stride you make,
Every deep breath you take,
You keep on soldiering on.
Although the battle is ever fierce,
Your body and your heart aches,
Never to hide, no need to shun,
Maybe feeling at times, you may need to outrun.
Yes, we say the battle is not ours.
And the way shall not be paved with beautiful
flowers,
And you have cried tears for hours upon hours,
When the rain clouds come, it pours not
showers.

You have taken this journey head-on,

with prayers and conviction, your Son lives on,

For your loved one's cause,

you placed your life on pause and nursed his

wounds and yours, your beautiful Son,

at present in this battle your number one.

All your offspring are in the fold

They have watched you fight on tirelessly,

brave and bold,

as a true Soldieress,

An elegant Empress.

Trying not to fold although everything feels

such a mess,

Acclamation and honour go out to you.

In all the past tribulations and mountains to

climb set into view,

Prayers still in place for what you are going

through.

Beautiful Soldieress, I know God is pleased with

you.

Dedicated to Donna and Lovell H and family...

THE FESTIVE SEASON
WITHOUT YOU

My heart feels so much heavier this Christmas
holiday,
For you are no longer here to share in this special
day.
The things you used to do,
There is still a place at the table set for you.

I'm now alone, having to face all these fears,
No shoulder to lean on,
Not even a telephone call,
Feeling as though,
I have crashed into a brick wall.

The heartbreak is unbearable,
No one understands Mom,
Not having you here to hold my hand,
To care and to worry about me.
At this present time, no longer do I feel free,
Our times together were as precious as gold,

But living without you has definitely been cold.

Unforgiving, unclear are the hands of time,

If they could turn back, I would gladly again

make you mine.

PANIC ATTACKS

Since Mom has died,

How much I have cried,

Until my eyeballs,

Are completely dried,

And really, I can't cry anymore,

My heart feels as though it has hit the floor.

Gathered are some feelings,

Of extreme anxiety,

When they take a hold of me,

I can't even breathe or even see.

My chest becomes tight,

And I feel so scared,

Out of reach, unprepared.

Pouring out this fear is from nowhere.

The breaths are shallow,

Coming rapidly in outward gasps,

Truly feeling to me like having a heart attack.

It seems hard to swallow,

My throat feels locked and dry,

My body tenses, I feel completely lost,

Shallow breaths gasping for air,
I try, needing to take control,
Slowing down my breathing, eyes are watering -
why?
Some musical notes in my head starting with a
treble cleft Raising up onto the ceiling.
My body is clammy, feeling so ridiculously hot,
I must now calm myself down,
Or I will miscount my breathing,
Then will stay lost aground,
Breathing deeply in and out,
I am becoming calmer,
Need to inhale, exhale deeply from inside out.
This anxiety sounds upon me so loud,
Wailing like a fire alarm,
Getting my breathing together, feelings need to
be calm.
Is this what is happening.... a panic attack?
Breathe slowly; this will stop me in my tracks.
Temperature lowered, feeling calm,
This fear removed, this process with control will
do you no harm.

FOR YOU ARE IN THE GENTLE BREEZE

The breeze within the trees reminds me of you
The gentleness of the breeze reminds me of the
things you used to do.
The trees swaying gently from left to right.
This is the way you wanted to live your life,
Doing the stuff pleasing to you.
You did not conform or play the game,
not seeking fortune
nor any fame.
Living your life carefree
With a gentle spirit to some degree.
Not allowing people or circumstance to change
you, taking the time to listen to sweet music
and dance.
And to drink sweet wine.
Time was of the essence
Life would have been your preference.

Walking on life's road forever with a smile

With the accolades of a semi-disciplined child.

When I peek over yonder, and I think of you,

I feel happy I was there to do what I could for you.

This was life, tinged with bouts of guilt and worry.

Your time here was not consumed by money.

You walked at a pace

Not in too much of a hurry. Suspending hope over our lives

Recognising right now, this is not a complete surprise.

The gentleness you propelled over our lives

Amidst the turmoil at times

Believing this has aided us to cope without you.

Not having your shoulder to cry on to help us to run this course and make it through.

Whisperings of you in the gentle breeze put my turbulent mind at ease.

So, as I stand, view, and look ahead,

I am still mad that you are dead.

The main fact that you have gone

Knowing that without you I must live on.

But when I feel that gentle breeze,
And hear the rustling of the trees,
I think of you and all the loving things you used
to do.
I smile a while and say,
"Mom, take your rest, for we love you,
but recognise that God loves you the best."
Whisperings of you in the gentle breeze
Puts my turbulent mind at ease.

THROUGH THE GLASS
WINDOW I STAND I STARE

Through the glass window, I stand, and I stare,

Remembering clearly,

That you are no longer, over there.

I am still patiently waiting for you,

Looking through the glass window,

As you used to do too.

In days gone by, you would look out for all of us.

If we took a long while to come over

You would surely cuss.

The tables have now turned, and I am still

patiently waiting for you.

Through the glass window

I am still longing to catch a glimpse in a side view.

This time of being, stagnant for too many years.

Going through tumultuous times, facing many of

my own fears.

Many days my cheeks awash with tears.

Through the glass window,

I continuously look,

Thinking of you, having inspired me to write

this book.

Dedicating this book of poetry, I am to you.

Knowing you encouraged me, telling me how

well I would do.

I am devoting this in full respect and honour of

you alone.

Recognising all the heartbreak that you went

through.

I wholly and solely with my eyes full of tears,

heart full of woe.

Sorrow filled words; I didn't want to let you go.

...Dedicated to My Mom... I Love You...

WELL-BEING WATERFALL

The well-being waterfall
Flowing with life,
Being in control of any trouble or strife,
No matter what trials
Will approach.
Do not become subdued.
Take each trial from scratch,
Buy a new pair of shoes.
Your well-being waterfall
Needs to overflow,
With peace, ambience, and tranquillity
And an abundance of joy.
Breathing deeply,
Relaxing within,
Feeling invigorated
From the outside in.
Taking the stress levels
Down and flushing out,
Removing anger or the need to shout.
The peace and radiance
That one will feel,
Is something to be shared,
That no one can steal.

Keeping that never-ending flow, pass the
message on to your friends,
Colleagues and loved ones,
They will thank you for letting them know.
This is the new normal,
Healing hands channelling positive energy,
The healing touch.
Conveys from a clean vessel, blessing from you
to me,
Promoting your physical, mental, and spiritual
wealth,
All by restoring your inner health.
Touch is an important part of our loving
chemistry,
Bringing about warmth and sensual energy.
Embracing your loved one with both hands,
Supporting someone who is exposed to the
extremities.
That life demands.
Being empathetic, showing sensitivity,
Allowing the alleviation of stress and anxiety,
The spiritual flow regulated to rejuvenate and
empower.
Taking time out maybe to take an invigorating
shower,
In the well-being waterfall
Flowing with life
Being in control of any trouble or strife.

RELIVING THE MEMORY TO RELIEVE THE PAIN

1st Year
To re-live the memory
To relieve the pain
Today is the day we do it all over again.
To remember you in the hospital bed
To think of this now, it hurts my head.
To close my two eyes
And envision you there
Leaves my heart in utter despair.
No one could help only for us to stop, drop and stare
to stop the world,
to drop a tear,
To stare at you and say a secret prayer,
to care for you,
to love you so,
to have no choice,
but to watch you go,
To watch the monitor every day,
to stay strong, that's all they could say,

To question the nurses and doctor too,
to place you in their hands,
thinking they will know what to do,
To find out later, that this was not true,
to know that I do not desire to be consoled,
To know that I could easily lose all self-control,
To know that I must handle my grief,
to make sure that I do not bury myself currently,
out of my loved one's reach.

2nd Year

The second year that you have gone,
I visited your resting place, yesterday MUM.
Planting flowers there what a beautiful display.
It's been 2 years now, but I'm struggling to get on,
Still can't believe that you have gone.
I keep on trying to so-called get by,
But my eyes still automatically begin to cry.
In this month of March, I become more lost,
For after this much time, there is still a huge cost.
The price for you not being here,
Is way too much for me to bear,
Still wondering why each and every day,
You were the one that death took away.

FOUGHT A BATTLE FROM A TENDER AGE

Fighting every day,

The battle seems to always be on.

Although it has already been won,

This feels to be an uphill climb,

Holding on tight trying not to lose my mind.

I always needed to fight for you,

Believing that is what I was called to do.

Now that you have gone,

Someone told me it's time now for me to move on.

How can that advice be?

If there is no you, then how can there be me?

My life had been constructed around yours,

Now you are not here; I cannot even close the
doors.

Knowing that my life is now way different from
before.

No way to delete the years,
Or bring about a pause.

From a tender age, I learnt to fight.
For you with all my might.
You experienced, and you suffered an
abundance of pain.
The strength you showed to me still remains.

I took this fight on to protect you,
In every aspect of life that I know you went
through.
I accepted different kinds of a breakthrough,
Throughout all, I could never neglect you.

I will never ever forget you and the grief that
stressed you.
I will have to release this fight now,
And say goodnight, although.
I do not know how to live on without you.

MEN'S HEARTS BREAK TOO

Our men have been broken,

Damaged and bruised.

They are seeking love, sustenance,

And a decent plate of food.

Their hearts have been damaged,

At times they can be rude.

We have been designed differently.

Acting angrily when they too have been bruised.

We ladies will talk and share our emotions with
a friend.

Our men will keep it all inside and burn until the
bitter end.

Let us show them patience and offer kindness
and show more.

of our Love.

This section can be difficult to navigate

Starting early there is no ability to turn up late

We too, are unprepared, lay it all on the table,

Easier to keep to task when both are able

The problem is easier once it is shared.

Not such a burden when the problem is aired

The brokenness is not always apparent, not always in your face.

Take time to speak.

For at times men show strength but are inside feeling weak

These issues are not easy if you are in any haste.

For their hearts are broken in places and too have damaged space.

This can become evidently formed, leaving scars and traces and unopened doors.

We are all not the same.

Please do not shut them out, this is what relationships are all about.

Be not fuelled by anger, malice, and washed away with doubt,

Let him know "Look, I am still here,

I am not going anywhere."

Try to firstly be a good friend

Someone hurt them before you came

The heartbreak can also leave damage on the brain,

Some never taking the time not to point the finger in blame

The label reads FRAGILE... HANDLE WITH CARE!

Hearts broken for this part of the journey, somewhat unprepared.

For Men may at times be feeling unstable.

They try to give love in times when unable

Healing is for all, and this can take time.

To prepare the heart, the soul, the mind

Sometimes much love is not left, once bereft

The vitals have been scarred, damaged,

from within uncared for, unkempt, ravaged.

Take their manly design into consideration,
let them handle their own frustration.

And let healing for them sink in.

This will happen within their own skin.

Travelling on the in road of this journey together,

Both with love and patience can overcome the
heartbreak and withstand any stormy weather.

THE PURSUIT FOR
HAPPY-NESS

In pursuit of money,
Entanglement can occur within the pursuit of
happy-ness.
This can result in a great loss of self.
A great loss of family, and no desire for friends,
The salary is high,
Love and morality are low.
Until you find yourself there, you will never,
truly know.
Working every hour that God sends,
No time for loved ones, family or even friends.
If the pursuit of money becomes your life ambition,
This could destroy your character losing all
inhibitions.
Awaken in the morning,
Money on your mind.
At the close of the evening,
No time to think of yourself and be kind
Got to keep on going,

Heading for the money to fill to the brink.

Not time to make a visit,

Or take time to see a friend. In the pursuit of money,

Your happy-ness will end.

OUR STRONG TOWER OF HONOUR AND STRENGTH

To continue your life, without us in it,
I believe he must have to give us a thought, for
even one minute.
I wonder if there is any guilt for leaving us,
On this, there shall be no more grieving,
Fatherless woman, of which I am,
This journey can be the downfall for a woman.
I am me, for this I am blessed, taking on a ton
load of stress.

Gained great strength from the mess my Father
left,
My mother was our strong tower of honour and
strength.
Which she showed to us amidst a great
abundance of distress,
Standing bold, showing brave,

I believe that is why she loved to rave (to de-
stress),
Raising her offspring to be no man's slave.

*In a home of much love, joy, tears, laughter,
amidst some fears*
With much fun maybe, some would have been
amazed,
We may not have had many things,
Not an abundance of toys, games, no diamond
rings,
But as happy, as happy ever after.
If my mother were alive, she would have been
awarded a BAFTA,
No acting, all real,
No one knew the pain she had to endure and
feel.

By such an influential queen,
But for our Father's absence had been felt,
Due to our mother, not in the best of health.
In hospital, she spent a great deal of time.

The stress of life aided her decline.

Whilst I learnt how to smile,

Behind a broken heart and saddened eyes,

Still, he chose to vacate our space,

He found himself another place,

A different family he chose for himself.

This was one of the lowest of blows for me,

But Mother showed us great care,

Aiding my spirit to be set free.

THOUGHTS OF YOU IN THE
BLACK OF THE NIGHT

In the black of the night,
I see your face,
Quickly, remembering you have gone on from
this place,
In my heart an empty space, that nothing can
replace.

In the still of the night
I wake and recount my dream of you,
Longing for you to stay within my view,
Thinking that your time for return is long overdue.

In the midst of the dawn
I long for your daily call to ask,
"how are you all?"
With patience, I anticipate this,
Then I fall asleep and tell myself, you,
I have missed.

In the morning light, I open my eyes
Wandering why tricks are playing with my mind,
Pondering that you are really WAITING at home,

Then rapidly my thoughts are shattered in a minute
When I realise this is it,
I am in bits.
When the truth of the reality hits,
Realising that you,
I will forever miss.
Undisputed!!!

CHECKING BACK INTO LIFE AND LETTING GO

Beginning to check back into life
To create something that feels normal, right,
If this is my 5 star hotel
I would like this to be comfortable, happy and well.
For, at present, I feel like I have visited hell.
The plastic smile can be glossed on and off,
Once you take a sip from life's champagne glass,
to swallow then, its flavour is lost,
Nothing to savour for later on the flavour has gone
Having experienced a broken heart and broken dreams,
Bursting at the well-embroidered seams,
Allowing you to place your feet in my fluffy slippers to see how they feel,
The removal of my rose-tinted glasses for you to try on and reveal exactly what I mean.
Lying on my memory foam mattress
This is the place I lay down with my own stress,

Snuggled deeply between two pillows
My heart droops like a weeping willow,
Heavy laden with woe
Which way should I turn, shall I stay, or should I go?

Having experienced a broken heart and many broken dreams, Bursting at the well-embroidered seams,
Letting you place your feet in my slippers to see how they feel, Removal of my rose-tinted glasses for you to try on and view.
Feeling burnt out from overuse,
Take the time to self-evaluate,
Tell yourself the honest truth, for today is for today,
And tomorrow is for tomorrow.
Take a moment to erase away your tears, embracing.
Then let go of your sorrow, never wasted
Don't keep forever, or it will never leave,
Be honest about who you are and what you believe.
The person you are seeking is around the corner not too far,

At the end of your sleeve,

Place the key card on the table. Life can be good if you are able.

Checking out is still no longer an option,

So, choose wisely which way to go,

For you know the hustle, but need to choose the flow,

With no need to inflict hurt upon yourself,

This is not 100% great quality for your health.

Many dreams have been broken, hearts too,

So now it's time to purchase a brand-new pair of walking shoes,

Black, shiny with or without a bow, to continue on your journey

Now it's time to dust them off and leave the past behind.

Check back into life by letting go...

IF TODAY WAS MY LAST DAY

How would I feel?

Would I request to eat my favourite meal?

Would I visit my loved ones to let them, see?

How very much they mean to me?

Would I kiss and hug them tight to show them much care?

Then ponder on the times when I would not be near.

Would I share with them my secrets, with nothing to hide?

And chose to pack away my selfish pride?

I Would love up my daughters, and love up my sons,

And love and embrace my grand ones,

Then also, love up my God-given ones.

Would we talk all morning and laugh all night,

Turning the music up high to aid us in our sorrowful strife?

Would I then choose not to leave and share my truth?

Knowing the voice of my Father's calling would render no reproof,

Would I do my uttermost to make things right?

With my brothers, my sister, my friends, and foe sparing the time to reunite,

Would I feel comfortable knowing I would have to go?

To, visit me early, before it's too late,

And there was no promise for tomorrow,

As this journey could be easily shortened according to my fate.

Would my decision be early, on time, but not is too late?

Telling them you love them, your family, and friends,

'cause none of us are perfect,

and we all will have an undisclosed time to separate.

Tell me you love me, as I will tell you,

As life's journey can be a challenge,

I know you have felt it too.

Do not be too disheartened or openly dismayed.

Experiments will come with loss, feelings of
being betrayed,

For life is still fruitful and love has been kind,

Having to hold you all in the depths of my mind.

So, I thank my Creator for it would have all
been blissful, fun;

hopefully, the next round of love

Will come on repeat, and in round two again you
will all be my number one.

Dedicated to my five children KTTSS With Love

SHEILA {PANIC MODE}

Sheila, I really miss you,

Sheila, I really do,

Sheila, you mean the world to me

Sheila, there is no meaning to this without you.

Sheila, now that you have gone I can well and truly see

Sheila, I think of you constantly.

Sheila, you mean the world to me,

Sheila in the morning light

Before I open my eyes.

I awaken and to my surprise,

Sheila, you bid me farewell and said your final goodbyes,

Sheila, I need to see your face one more time

Sheila, your heart is fused with mine.

Sheila, where are you now?

Sheila, how am I living without you? I can't tell you how.

Sheila, can you see me?

If so, I am scared, but

I hope your spirit has been set free.

Sheila, I miss your touch and your smell,

Sheila, I miss you too much, I know this feeling so well.

Sheila, I need you now.

Sheila, I am living without you, I can't tell you how.

Sheila, my Mom and my best friend

Sheila, I am still missing you, and I can't pretend.

Sheila, I L.O.V.E you now until the END.

Sheila, I L.O.V.E you now until the END.

TO BREAK THE HEART OF A BROKEN WO-MAN

Saddened by the fact that the LOVE you turn to
can be the hurt you receive,
Hoping that we all can gain forgiveness before
we leave,
The hurt you hand out is the part on display,
Thinking on this, I wept again too much today.
To have broken an already broken heart, in such
a way,
Bringing me up then breaking me down again,
the very next day.
I am at times lost for words, in a swirl of dismay,
You turned my smile into a frown.
Not sure what I am to believe,
Are you supposed to be a friend, or did you
come to deceive?
Riding high upon the cloud,
Gaining validation from you, feeling almost proud,
Then you pulled the rug from under my feet,

Allowing me to again to experience the depths
and barriers of grief.

Just because you are feeling down,
I will not allow you to steal my well-earned
golden crown.

I feel blessed to be able to put my feelings out
on display,
I am an empathetical being, that is my way.

You have held my heart within both your palms,
Red flag, raise the alarms,
You then squeezed it tightly, as you felt life
commands,

To replicate your special effects,
Not recognising that this is sheer neglect.

Placing the rugged noose around my neck,
To allow me to squirm, to scream and to sweat.

Please do not tell me that this was your master
plan,
To break the broken heart of a broken wo-man.

WEATHERING THE STORMS OF LIFE

We can walk this life together, weathering many
storms.
When all is done, we can lay in one another's arms.
Stay strong, Be blessed,
Stand strong through these life tests.
Aid each other in our strife,
Hold steadfast on the journey, like man and wife.
Spread our existence over this place,
As we turn over, we see one another's face.
Through sickness, blessings, good gifts and woe,
We know one day, one of us will have to go (first).
That is how the seed was sown,
We know this, for we have watched the flowers
grow.
To live, to die
To laugh to love,
Showered down with the knowledge, wisdom and
understanding.
The weather changes, as do the seasons,

We know we have been blessed with this life for
different reasons,
Although at times we are unsure what to do,
No matter what, let the positivity flow essentially
through.
Winter comes, the time is cold,
Give God thanks for making us bold.
Autumn comes, then the leaves on the trees die,
Floating away, then we wonder why.
Many times, tears fall from our eyes,
Springtime brings joy to our hearts,
Each day we live, God allows us a brand-new start.
The Summertime comes and brings with it
sunshine,
Then the rays bellow down, helping to clear,
elevate our minds
Our hearts and hands,
To bring touch to others
With the warmth of the rays of the weather,
Embracing one another,
Weathering the storms of life forever, together.
For life is the most beautiful part in the storm,
We shall live in love and pray to be free from harm.

I MISS YOU SO MUCH/
LOVE STORY

I miss you so much.
How much you will never know.
Although you're away from me
My love has grown ten thousand folds.

I know now you will never see how much you
really mean to me,
But now that you are free, I am beginning to see
Just how very much you meant to me.

This road has been so long, my heart has been
aching, thinking of your home going, my knees
are uncontrollably shaking, I sit down with
myself, debating, The rest of our lives
undoubtedly anticipating.

These long DAYS and NIGHTS without you,
But your voice over the telephone got me
through, these days are long, the nights are TOO,
But I believe it will be longer without you.

I pray nightly that we will remain strong.
As for you, the time must seem so long,
So, hold the faith so that we can be together,
Hoping that our lives will bind again, never to
be unbound forever.

TO CLIP MY WINGS

You try to hold me down so that we will tussle,
Then I strive to become free,
That is due to the freedom of spirit, which lives
within me.

My wingspan opens immensely wide,
In order to enable me to fly,
Soaring above the cloud's, way up high.
Looking down upon my life,
To see the fragmented shackles scattered
throughout the strife,
Enabling me to pick my life up from the ground.

No longer shall I reside here,
For upon myself I place more love and intensity
of care,
You long to hold me down, in order to clip my
wings,
But now that I see clearly throughout all things,
These wings I've been blessed with are mine for
my life.

No more shackles around my neck,
Not willing to bear any more disrespect,

Today I live and learn for brighter tomorrows,
Never to own my pain or embrace any more
sorrow.

Written about a man who can't embrace a
woman's free-spirited ways

SUMMER IS HERE

To Grandma {nanny Sheila}

Summer is here!!

School is out!!

All the children laugh, cheer and shout.

No more classes,

Or early morning trundle,

No more mommy hollering to 'wake up,'

Allowed to stay in bed in a happy bundle.

Long days,

Even longer nights,

Summer holidays make life bright.

Days out to the beach, picnics too,

There are lots of fun things for all to do.

Trips to the parks,

Swinging on the swings,

Viewing all the squirrels and natures birds, with

colourful wings, visiting the animals at the zoo,

With friends and family, all invited too.

Movies, popcorn, candy floss,

Time filled up; school thoughts may be lost.

The moments quickly pass by when you're

having fun,

Summer's here, looking forward to the sun.

Picking pretty flowers,

Buying gorgeous fruits,

Going through the Helter-Skelter, flying down

the shoot,

Ice cream sundaes,

Fruit smoothies too,

Mmm, I can't wait for the taste test .... can you?

Summer is here,

Summer is fun,

We would have been hanging out with our

beautiful grandma this Summer,

But sadly, she has now passed on.

Missing you Zy, Lay and Keiah with Love x

Written and dedicated to my three beautiful
grandchildren

LIFE BEGINS WITH A PALLET OF PAINTS

Life begins with a pallet of paints.
The joy and subtlety of the colours creating the
scene shall be truly quaint.
With the gentle hum in a harmonious song,
Within a long, lazy day, when nothing goes wrong.
Handling the paintbrush with ingenuity,
To paint your vision vicariously
Within this picture, only fully, open, eyes will
have that unique vision to see,
The softness of this genuine artistry, there shall
be no mistake adding in peaks and flows,
Free love shall reciprocate from the depths and
colours of the deep blue sea.
Created within one's own mind's eye, upon the
whiteness of a clean canvas,
Without disguise but new to us, the thoughts of
this shall stir up new emotions on the inside.
Some from memories can be horrendous,
deep set with pride,

The scene simply unique and stupendous.

Once created, the artistic imagery will render you speechless,

For the picture is sculpted out of the heartache transformed into shades,

Following gently with turquoise peaks and charcoal curves,

Twisting through the mind and visions of your own story, and swerves.

Heralded loudly for all to wonder and glory,

The details are dark, painted slowly, but can be gory.

Superbly etched frozen, into a winter's day tale,

Painted patiently in front of an open, log fire - pulling from your thoughts and visions the churning red,

Orange embers laying upon the black ash, the burning smell shall curtail the story all the way back.

To set the scene

Illustrated on canvas of love between two people that shall successfully prevail.

This artistic image has now been creatively formed, never to die but still will remain.

Finding a unique way to paint the love within the pain.

On the blank canvas, a picturesque scene
Created from the pallet of colourful paint,
colouring in your dreams.
The scene could be swirly pink, wonderful or yellow and green.
Use the grey colour to create the gloomy state.

This is your canvas, and this is your colourful pallet of paints,
This is your story artistically, with life's pallet paint.

'C' THE WAY IN THE DARK

You made your way into our lives and made
your mark,
Plunging our friends and family into the depths
of the dark.
Ruining dreams, blighting our futures,
If I had my way and could 'C' you,
I would most definitely shoot ya.
Like a roaring river, you gushed right in,
Seeping into the blood vessels, settling yourself
within.
Like a lion with a wide-open jaw,
With sharp teeth to rip the skin and settle a score.
You entered in, to take your place,
To take our Mom at a selfishly, rapid pace.
Shuffling the pack of our existence,
Whilst we battle to cope, from the nearest
distance.
The dance of death, you have brought to us,
No time to fight or make a fuss.
Being there to comfort our loved one,
For, in days to weeks, they could be gone.
Memories of our fun-filled times,

At any length, nearly blowing our minds,
making no sense.

There is no time to gird our hearts beyond a
protective, wooden fence.

*Dedicated to Jo Brown and family in loving
memory of Kathy.*

ANGELS DISGUISED AS FRIENDS

Truly you are dear to me
Kind, loving, beautiful and somewhat carefree.
Reaching out to me in my time of need
In many ways being there to support me.
Helping me to remember to breathe,
Whether to laugh, cry, dance, or sing.
In the joys of friendship, you now bring
My angels are disguised as friends.
As we go on in life on our sweet way,
Things befall us on a day-to-day.
We grumble, we cry, we worry and we fret
And forget to recall that our Creator has not left
us yet.
He sent an angel to surround us in need
He does it out of His Love for us.... yes indeed!!

My angels are disguised as friends
So, at times when I'm feeling blue,
I must remember He only sends a few,
And realise that
He sent me to also be a wonderful friend to you.
My angels are disguised as friends.

Dedicated to my Angels, my Friends x

IN THE PARK AMONGST THE PIGEON'S MOMENT

I remember when you would sit at the local park,
Amongst the pigeons gathering your own
thoughts in the dark,
At that time, I didn't understand why,
But now you have gone, and I think of that time,
often I cry,
I realise that some of your un-tailored journey,
May have walked you out of his life too early.

Seeking a place of solitude,
No thoughts to share,
In that safe haven, you craved alone time there,
No one to interrupt your quiet space,
Believing now, the burdens were heavy,
Grabbing time, but not having plenty,
To meditate, to let the thoughts empty,
In order to relieve your mind,
For life had been so unkind, almost seemed like
a century.

Just a short while to let things go,
Here now I stand, now I definitely know,
When life fills your cup up to the brim,
And you're overwhelmed, predicting to sink or swim.
Grabbing a lifejacket is the only way,
Not allowing your life to decay,
Harshly put,
Harshly felt,
This was your way to preserve your life,
conducive to your health.

Seeking a place of solitude,
No thoughts to share,
In that safe haven, you craved alone time there,
No one to interrupt your quiet space,
Believing now, the burdens were heavy,
Grabbing time, but not having plenty
To meditate, to let the thoughts empty,
In order to relieve your mind,
For life had been so unkind, almost seemed like a century.

All may have experienced this park, amongst the pigeon's moment,
Frightened for our own life is impinging part of the component,
At this time remembering, you are not alone,
Reach out to someone who loves you and can walk you home.

"Thinking on mom experiencing the dark episodes in her life."
I would walk my mom home!!!

LIFE HAS A SPIRITUAL MEANING

Embracing life as a spiritual being,

Enhances and enriches your inner feeling.

Removing all negative energies,

Assisting to detain all who commit felonies.

Watching the swaying of trees, waving of the
waves in the seas,

Blowing and flowing with a natural, mystical ease.

Not a worry, without a care,

Remaining rooted, right there.

Using touch, taste, sight and smell,

All-natural components, so that you can tell.

Who is around? How do they feel? Are they fake?
Or are they real?

Spiritual equilibrium is a gift from within,

Aspiring to get this into balance,

This can be an overwhelming challenge,

A necessity to be focussed upon,

For without this in-balance, being stuck, unable to move along,

Hold this spirituality in your hands,

Don't let go even when life commands.

Find yourself in a tranquil space,

Take your time, no need for haste.

Inhale in,

Exhale out,

Think on what this spiritual concept, called life, is all about, Mel's creation.

A RIVER OF TEARS

A river of tears,
With a heart full of fears,
Nowhere to run,
Feeling that no one cares,
Opening my eyes,
You are no longer there.
Reaching out to touch you,
To inhale the aroma of your perfume in the air,
Then, the sadness and gloom bring me to despair.
The cloak of darkness engulfs my mind,
Visiting your graveside,
Where your body now lies,
As I sit next to this dwelling,
A river of tears rolls down my face,
Whilst I mourn, your spirit vacates.
I bid you a sweet farewell, good night,
As you have left, the river of tears now fills this
place,
A river of tears,
With a heart full of fears,
Nowhere to run,
Feeling that no one cares,
Opening my eyes,
You are no longer there.

BEING THANKFUL

As the roses die, the petals wither.

As the roses die, the petals wither,
We love the gift but do not embrace the giver.

At the mountain peak, we stand in life,
Not taking the time to treat our loved ones right.
As the winds blow triumphantly,
Underestimating the human mind, as the ability
to flow free,
As the harpist strums the strings, in an
ensemble' melody,
We misinterpret, that we shall leave this place
one day.
As the sun rises at dawn,
Appreciation of the morning clock alarm, As the
embers of the fire glow,
We wonder if we can steer the way our journey
will go.
As we listen to the melodious laughter of small
children,

We realise that they may flee the nest one day,

As we watch the rivers peaceably flow,

We have the choice to say Yes or say No,

To learn whether to love, to live, to laugh or to grow.

This is most of the story.

Being thankful for all, by giving the Almighty the glory,

For there is nothing new under the sun,

Where we start is where we've begun,

As the roses die and the petals wither,

We love the gift but need to be eternally thankful to the giver.

TIME

Time has no regard or respect for any human being...

Time is its own master; we can never be above time...

Time has its own time...

The time we're all living in is taking us closer to death...

Time is not your own, or controlled by any person, or being...

There will be a time to live and a time to die...

Time is universal, we can be anywhere in time...

We can certainly be, on our own time...

For time is limitless...

That's why there are no boundaries to time...

Time is independent of its own time.

Time has a unique purpose...

Every human has his, or her own time...

By K Phillips

NO BED OF ROSES

Life at times has been no bed of roses,

No Butterfly covered bedding, no tiptoeing

through the Posies. Life at times has been

unattractively grim,

Although, fully grateful for the skin I've been

blended within.

Life at times has been a tug of war,

Many times, facing struggles through an

unlocked door.

Scenes that could have rocked my core,

Aiding me to give a great deal to receive less,

not more,

This has been a harsh reality, I'm sure.

Life at times can be changed from the outside in,

Not always focusing solely on the grim.

Being humble,

Taking heed,

Not always centralising your wants over your

needs.

Life for all is truly a blessing,

Take the time out in order to learn from life's
lessons. Harnessing the wealth of positives,
At greater lengths and speed,
Promoting, not to be overhauled by wealth or
greed.

FALLEN OUT WITH THE
WORLD AS A LITTLE GIRL

Wondering if I had fallen out of love with the
world when I was just a little girl?
When I would sit in the grass making daisy
chains, picking dandelion flowers, in the fields
behind my home in the sunshine rays.
And practice cartwheels, falling flat upon my
back.
My dreams at that time were all vivid and real,
At the time they came, with a guaranteed LOVE
imprinted seal,
With stamped approval, and a radiant smile
Skipping throughout as a disciplined child.
Knowing now that my family life had been
broken from the start,
At the time, life was ruled by my innocent heart,
Loving everyone and everything
One day, I realised my dad did not provide my
Mom with a wedding ring.
The thought was so puzzling to me,
But I carried on naïve, happy, and carefree,
My love for the world was gently changing,
To tell you why, is such a strange thing,

118

Maybe that was when people began to let me
down,
And those who were supposed to care for me
were just not around.
Recognising adults did not always speak the
truth,
My trust for grown-ups started to falter as a
youth.
Continuing my journey throughout this life,
Still, some segments were just not right.
Seeing many with way too much and noticing
others with nothing.
Life started showing signs, that it was getting
tough,
My Mom not always herself having enough.
Yet she never, ever gave up
Always continuing to try
At an early age, my eyes watched her as she
would cry.
Never as a child was, I put to bed hungry,
This was not an option given by my mommy.
Going to school every day,
I know that she would daily pray.
From a little girl inside my mind,
the life I had started to realign.
Unfortunately, this idea was too strange,
that wasn't how it was supposed to be arranged

We have no control in which way the wind blows,
So, the dreams and plans of which I made,
Did not come to pass, of this I'm afraid.
The blueprint was not made by me,
There was another I believe, designed for me to be.
So, as for me falling out of love with the world, when I was just a little girl,
As a grown woman now, I am seeking to find the beauty of the oyster within the pearl,
The key to life is learning there is no need to walk alone in this whole wide world,
Dreams are made for little girls to have, with both hands to hold and grab.
At times you need to clasp your hands, recognising that life has great and pressing demands.
Taking the time to self-reflect on, the little girl that fell out with the world now existing without her mom.
And is still seeking to find the pearl,
Now being a grown-up woman recognising that same little girl.

AN EMPTY SPACE WITHIN MY HEART

The nights are dark,

The cold draws nigh.

My beloved has gone, never a moment to say
goodbye.

My soul feels lost, as I close the blinds,

With only you and our lost love daily on my
mind.

I wrap up warm, ever to think of you,

Wondering how I will make it through.

I feel your spirit near, although far apart,

There is an empty place within my heart.

TO LABOUR IN LOVE TO BRING FORTH MY CHILDREN

When a mother gives birth to her precious gift of a child, this brings her to the closest point to death in life.

Bringing forth those blessings, ones so meek and mild, a true state and evidence that life makes sense, embracing that magnificent moment and what comes next.

The inner sanctuary awakens in order to house this new life, then into labour to bore her blessings, that's a splendid choice.

Blood pressure up, heart rate stressing,
To bring her trueness of love,
Which is filled with a richness of blessing.
This is a testimony within a testimony,
This is the beginning of a magnificent love story,
to the Almighty Father, we give all the glory,

An amazing sacrifice,
A visual of life CREATED, inside of a life story.

Whether amidst immense happiness, or
unbearable pain,
A gift given from within, with no time to refrain.
From the inner core of a Mother's soul,
Throughout the contours in a mother's mind.
The blood running into the deepest caverns of
the heart,
To bring forth and nurture, a brand-new start.
Bringing this unique, innocent and precious life
into being,
Generating an aura with such a true and
everlasting meaning.

When a mother bores a child, that is an intense,
emotionally charged feeling,
Smiling into a TINY, newly lived-in face,
The sheer meekness and innocence fuelled by
LOVE and grace.

Looking on beyond the scenes,
Only having to venture there, to visualise what
was once in her dreams,
The depth and intensity of this tranquil place,
Possibly envisaging a body within the outer space.
To convey with sheer power, of the greatest
strength,
To deactivate the negative concepts of the brain
at any length.

To climb this mountainous 100-foot picket fence,
This is in no way a stroll in the park,
The toll on one can come across, ultimately stark.
Lying there momentarily lost within the pitches
of the dark.
Nowhere else to go.

The travail on the body is sharper than a two-
edged sword,
Once over deserving, of one billion rounds of
applause, Contracting muscles with a second-
by-second blow.

The depths of intensity in pain,

Brings a weird sense of relief into the brain.

To bring forth the pitter-patter of those tiny feet,

And the sounds of that tiny heartbeat.

That smell of a brand-new birth, blessed onto you,

For new life, is what it's called to do.

This labour of love can tear down reinforced
enemy walls,

Within that gushing sound of Niagara Falls.

When a mother gives birth to her precious child,

Her whole world and body takes a magnificent
and treacherous roller coaster ride.

To create this immaculate, glorious, special gift,

The love of that moment is constant and swift.

Dedicated to my five children

THE HEART SHOULD BE LIVING

The heart is an organ filled with an abundance
of love, used to listen, touch, and heal,
Imprinted with a permanent lip kissed seal.
Recreating sound waves that are bouncing back,
Using them wisely, never to lack.
These messages highlighted are actually real,
Shining your love light across an open
battlefield.
As the gentleness of a lullaby comforts one,
within a soothing motion,
The waves cascading back and forth likened to
the sounds of the jasmine-jade ocean.
Showing lasting love succumbing to devotion,
And not being driven away by your own
distressing emotion.
The heart has the elements to exhume love,
In tune with the mind,

To distribute beauty from above
Being able to be gentle and kind.
Listening to your inner feelings,
Hearing the echoes from your heart,
Followed by then, the love will impart.
Not wearing your heart, upon your sleeve,
Wrapping wisdom tightly, to protect all of these

KATHY

"Always ferocious and always strong...
The Queen of the Ghetto all her days long."
The pressure is seeking to penetrate my heart,
At the thought of knowing, you will depart.
Right in front of our very eyes,
Not a sought-after surprise.
We know in life we rise, yet we too can fall,
When we hear the harken of His gentle call.
Whether to hear it now or to hear it later
The celebration of your life we shall honour and
cater.
In this life, you knew of beautiful Love,
And in sickness, you felt the darkness of pain
Searching for the peace of a Dove
Comfort and peace became your fortress,
We show gladness as you chose to fight this.
Together we stand to honour you
And all that life carried you through
For our Love will stay forever the same
Together in life, we shall remain

To allow for your passage to be ever so slight
With Our Love and God's grace, we bid you a
sweet and peaceful

GOODNIGHT

Dedicated to Kathy Brown {Jo's Mom}

{Healing}

{Healing}, is a true and relevant feeling,
Encircling thoughts all around and about you,
still revealing, A journey of passage,
From a position of great pain,
The battles that are faced, choosing to remain.
Death, divorce, illness and poverty,
Many impoverished people interjected into this
reality.
The outlook appears dark, one's outcome looks
stark, at the hearts centre, at the soul's core,
For *{Healing}*, is not projected via a revolving
door.
Although each and everyone's journey is
unique, your personal recovery,
should put on daily repeat.
To rebuild a relationship within oneself,
Recognising that *{Healing}*, is crucial to your
health.

For when *{Healing}*, comes, it flows like a glossy river, as long as you believe, faith will deliver, in times when you need to grieve.

Faith is required in abundance to bring you back up to speed, remembering to advocate and to deeply breathe.

This is a divine gift from our giver, deserving a plethora of applause.

For those in need of this tranquillity shall be overhauled, enabling a spiritual stop, pray and pause.

Positivity, throughout and roundabout, not allowing your life to be shrouded in any doubt.

Restoration is designed to heal from the inside out. Listen to the words coming from out of the mouth.

The stillness within this new equilibrium of space, to restore life's preservation at a transforming, health-inducing pace.

YOUR JOURNEY HAS COME TO AN END

Your journey has come to an end,
My Mom, my children's nan, and my best
friend. I did not want to say goodbye
But, now standing here with tears in my eyes
Each one that rolls down my cheek
In turn, is making my knees feel weak.

I watched you on that last day
Willing for you to awake, whilst I prayed,
I knew in my heart that this journey would tear
us apart. I felt this tugging within my heart
As I know now, I will not remain whole
Without you in my life to keep my soul.

How will I cope without you?
To see your beautiful eyes within your smiling
face. Touched by mercy saved by grace
What will we do without you?

Who will kiss us when we leave? How will we
cope?
How can we grieve?

The days will be short, the nights will be long.
Without the music of your sweet songs
We shall cry, we shall surely weep,
Never to have another torment-ridden less sleep.

Looking to the Lord to gain courage & strength
And ask him kindly to make your passage clear
Taking our angel home from out of her pain
Until one day to hopefully meet you again.

Our journey together has come to an untimely
end. My dear mother, my Queen & my friend.
I pray your arms I will feel embrace me once
more. This legacy that you leave with us is ours
to endure.

Sleep beloved angel Mother, Queen & friend

NOTE FROM THE AUTHOR

This journey has been an uphill struggle for me. To put this compilation of poems together, I have had to overcome an excess of hurdles.

Death of my Mom and loved ones, divorce, studying studies and leaving for work, the list goes on. At times I have felt as though it was too much for me to achieve alone. Sigh!!! But if not for the Grace of God. Jehovah Jireh, Prince of Peace, The Almighty Father and Creator, I am nowhere!

Family dying, friends too many times unable to see a breakthrough. But amidst it all, I kept on writing thankfully daily. At my desk, whilst on the phone wherever and whenever and by any means necessary. (Quote ... unquote)

I have never struggled to write down what I had to say, As I opened my eyes, I took hold of my pen starting on that day. Opening my heart, pen to paper and everything poured out, saving nothing for later. Having to write my thoughts down there and then {or else it would be lost forever, never to be heard again}.

I would be in the bathroom taking a shower, not highlighting the time, the minute or the hour, but when those words began to bounce in my head, I would need to clamber out to find a pen and paper to write them down instead.

Sometimes I would pen, other times I would voice, at times whether busy or not, I would have no choice, within my struggles on this day, a letter came to make a large impression on my way.

The heading underlined the word divorce, but to be honest, unsurprisingly, I was not distraught. Recognising this was another ploy to take me off course.

This, on top of everything, did not faze me; For life brings high and lows, not all to amaze, you see.

I have known this story well; I had become self-taught and never allowed it to kill or destroy or my spirit to quell. I recognised this as one more hurdle.

Too much thought would make my stomach curdle. I didn't choose to lose my head, for stress is out there, and I didn't want to end up unwell.

My therapy of choice was to pray, to reach my goal today and every day. To dedicate my words within a poetry book to my Dear Mom, who was there for me from my life be.
To signify her life's beautiful beginning and to seal her life's untimely end.

Although to this day, I still can't comprehend, The loss of my Mom and my best friend.

So, this is my sheer reason to continue my journey. This is my destiny, never late and not too early.

Melonie Phillips

www.marciampublishing.com